Pharmacists

by Karen Bush Gibson

Consultant:
Jann Skelton, Pharmacist
Senior Director, Professional Practice Development
American Pharmaceutical Association

Bridgestone Books
an imprint of Capstone Press
Mankato, Minnesota

Bridgestone Books are published by Capstone Press
151 Good Counsel Drive, P.O. Box 669, Mankato, Minnesota 56002
http://www.capstone-press.com

Library of Congress Cataloging-in-Publication Data
Gibson, Karen Bush.
     Pharmacists/by Karen Bush Gibson.
     p. cm.—(Community helpers)
     Includes bibliographical references and index.
     Summary: Introduces the work pharmacists do, the equipment and clothing
they use, the required education, and their importance to the communities they serve.
     ISBN 0-7368-0624-5
     1. Pharmacists—Juvenile literature. [1. Pharmacists. 2. Occupations.] I. Title.
II. Series.
RS92 .G53 2001
615'.1—dc21   00-023611

Editorial Credits
Sarah L. Schuette, editor; Timothy Halldin, cover designer; Katy Kudela,
     photo researcher

Photo Credits
David F. Clobes, 8
FPG International LLC/Jeff Kaufman, cover
Index Stock Imagery, 14
International Stock/Patrick Ramsey, 4, 12; Jay Thomas, 20
Unicorn Stock Photos/Jeff Greenberg, 6, 18; R. Nolan, 10; B.W. Hoffmann, 16

1 2 3 4 5 6 06 05 04 03 02 01

Table of Contents

Pharmacists

Pharmacists help people stay healthy. They prepare medicine for people who are sick. Pharmacists teach people about medicine. They work with doctors and scientists to make sure medicine works.

medicine
a drug used to
treat an illness

What Pharmacists Do

Pharmacists fill prescriptions. A prescription is an order for medicine from a doctor. Pharmacists show people how to take medicine. Some medicine needs to be taken with food or water. Pharmacists tell people about side effects.

side effects
the ways that some medicines can affect people

Where Pharmacists Work

Pharmacists work in drug stores or pharmacies. People go to pharmacies to pick up medicine. Pharmacists also work in hospitals and nursing homes.

Tools Pharmacists Use

Pharmacists use scales to measure and weigh medicines. They use computers to keep track of medical records and to learn about new medicines. Pharmacists sometimes use a blood pressure cuff to give blood pressure tests.

blood pressure test

a test used to find out how fast blood moves through a body

Skills Pharmacists Need

Pharmacists need good math skills to figure the correct dose of medicine for people. They also need science skills. Pharmacists need to clearly explain how medicines work. People depend on pharmacists to know about new medicines.

dose
an exact amount
of medicine

What Pharmacists Wear

Pharmacists wear clean and neat clothes. They sometimes wear lab coats over their clothes. Pharmacists often wear gloves and masks to keep medicines clean and safe.

Pharmacists and School

Pharmacists go to college to learn about medicine and different kinds of drugs. They learn about side effects. The students must pass tests on what they have learned.

college

a place where students study after high school

People Who Help Pharmacists

Doctors and nurses help pharmacists. They work together to find the right medicine for a patient. Scientists study how medicine affects people. They discover and make new medicines.

How Pharmacists Help Others

Pharmacists help people understand how to take prescriptions. They answer questions about medicine and side effects. Pharmacists help people get well and stay healthy.

Hands On: Growing Penicillin

Scientist Alexander Fleming discovered the medicine penicillin (pen-uh-SIL-uhn) in 1928. Penicillin is made from mold. You can see how mold grows.

What You Need

A glass jar with a lid
Orange or lemon slices
Small piece of bread
Water

What You Do

1. Dip the bread and the orange slices in water.
2. Put the bread and the orange slices inside the glass jar. Seal the jar with a lid.
3. Let the jar sit for a few days. Do not open the jar.
4. Watch for blue or green fuzzy mold to grow on the bread and fruit.
5. Throw the whole jar away after 2 weeks. Do not use the jar again.

Words to Know

college (KOL-ij)—a place where students study after high school

dose (DOHSS)—an exact amount of medicine

medicine (MED-uh-suhn)—a drug used to treat an illness

mold (MOHLD)—a fuzzy substance that sometimes grows on old food; the medicine penicillin is made from mold.

prescription (pri-SKRIP-shuhn)—an order for medicine from a doctor; a prescription tells the pharmacist what kind of medicine to give to a person.

side effects (SIDE uh-FEKTS)—the ways that some medicines can affect people

Read More

Romaine, Deborah S. *Health Care.* San Diego: Lucent Books, 2000.

Tames, Richard. *Penicillin: A Breakthrough in Medicine.* Point of Impact. Chicago: Heinemann Library, 2000.

Internet Sites

Pharmacist
http://stats.bls.gov/k12/html/sci_001.htm
Pharmacy and You
http://www.pharmacyandyou.org
What Does A Pharmacist Do?
http://www.webquarry.com/~lgfd/pharmcst.htm

Index